FERRARI SF90 STRADALE

BY KAITLYN DULING

EPIC

BELLWETHER MEDIA ›› MINNEAPOLIS, MN

EPIC BOOKS are no ordinary books. They burst with intense action, high-speed heroics, and shadows of the unknown. Are you ready for an Epic adventure?

This edition first published in 2024 by Bellwether Media, Inc.

No part of this publication may be reproduced in whole or in part without written permission of the publisher. For information regarding permission, write to Bellwether Media, Inc., Attention: Permissions Department, 6012 Blue Circle Drive, Minnetonka, MN 55343.

Library of Congress Cataloging-in-Publication Data

LC record for Ferrari SF90 Stradale available at: https://lccn.loc.gov/2023036155

Editor: Rachael Barnes   Designer: Jeffrey Kollock

Printed in the United States of America, North Mankato, MN.

TABLE OF CONTENTS

HYBRID HYPERCAR »

A driver unplugs the Ferrari SF90 Stradale. This **hybrid** car is charged up.

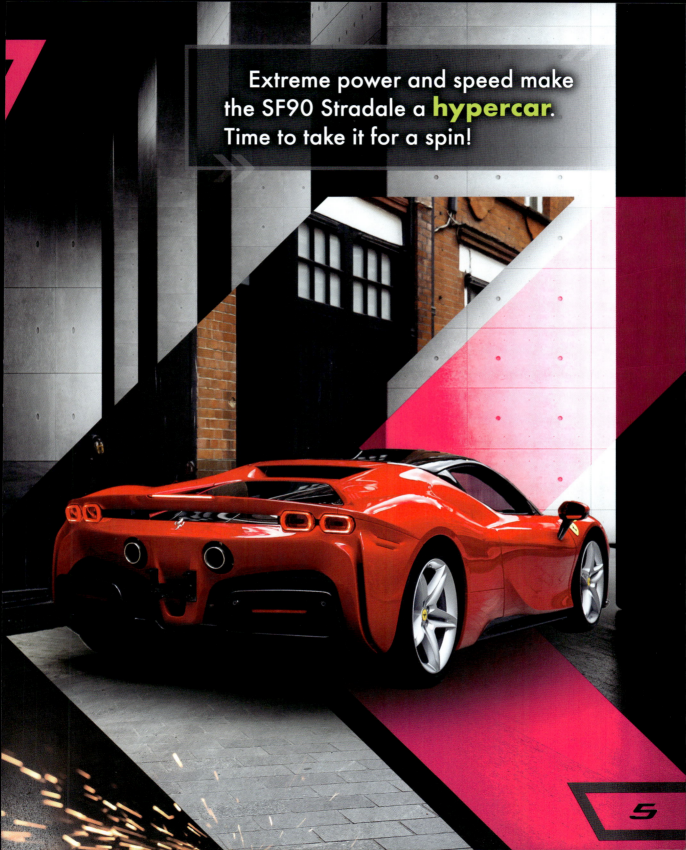

Extreme power and speed make the SF90 Stradale a **hypercar**. Time to take it for a spin!

ALL ABOUT THE SF90 STRADALE »

EARLY FERRARI RACE CAR

Ferrari was founded in Italy in the 1940s. At first, the company built race cars.

Today, Ferrari makes cars for **Formula One** races and for the road. The 250 GT and F40 are famous **models**.

F40

📍 WHERE IS IT MADE?

EUROPE

MARANELLO, ITALY

The SF90 Stradale was released in 2019. Its look was based on Ferrari race cars. It is Ferrari's fastest and most powerful road car. It speeds up to 60 miles (97 kilometers) per hour in just 2 seconds!

A FAMOUS NAME

SF90 honors the 90th year of Ferrari's racing team. The word *stradale* means "road" in Italian.

SF90 STRADALE BASICS

YEAR FIRST MADE 2019

COST starts around $530,000

HOW MANY MADE currently in production

FEATURES

large air intakes

C-shaped headlights

V8 engine

PARTS OF THE ›› SF90 STRADALE

V8 ENGINE

The SF90 Stradale is a plug-in hybrid car. It is powered by a **V8 engine** and three **electric motors**.

Each front wheel is powered by a motor.
A rear motor allows the car to reverse.

The SF90 Stradale has four drive modes. The eDrive mode uses only the electric motors. Hybrid mode uses the engine and motors. Performance mode is fast and charges the **battery**. Qualify mode is for maximum power!

ENGINE SPECS

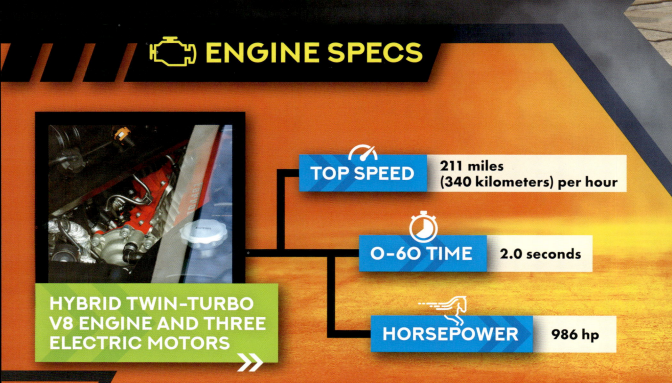

HYBRID TWIN-TURBO V8 ENGINE AND THREE ELECTRIC MOTORS

TOP SPEED — **211 miles (340 kilometers) per hour**

0–60 TIME — **2.0 seconds**

HORSEPOWER — **986 hp**

makes it **aerodynamic**.
Air moves over and under the car.

SIZE CHART

WIDTH 77.6 inches
(197.2 centimeters)

Powerful engines can get hot. Large **air intakes** bring air into the body. This cools the engine.

AIR INTAKE

HEIGHT 46.7 inches (118.6 centimeters)

LENGTH 185.4 inches (471 centimeters)

SF90 Stradale owners can choose from 25 different body colors!

SF90 STRADALE SPIDER

Owners can choose different options for the car. The SF90 Stradale Spider is a **convertible**.

The Assetto Fiorano package has lighter parts. It also adds a rear **spoiler** to help grip the road.

SPOILER

SF90 STRADALE
ASSETTO FIORANO

17

Inside, the SF90 Stradale looks like a race car! It has two low seats. Many controls are on the steering wheel.

LOW SEAT

READY, SET, GO!

Drivers tap a button on the steering wheel to start the SF90 Stradale!

START BUTTON

A **head-up display** shows information on the windshield. It helps drivers keep their eyes on the road!

THE SF90 STRADALE'S FUTURE »

Ferrari continues to build new models of the SF90 Stradale. The SF90 XX Stradale is faster. Another model will have over 1,300 **horsepower**. The company will continue to build electric cars. More plug-ins are on the way!

SF90 XX STRADALE SPIDER

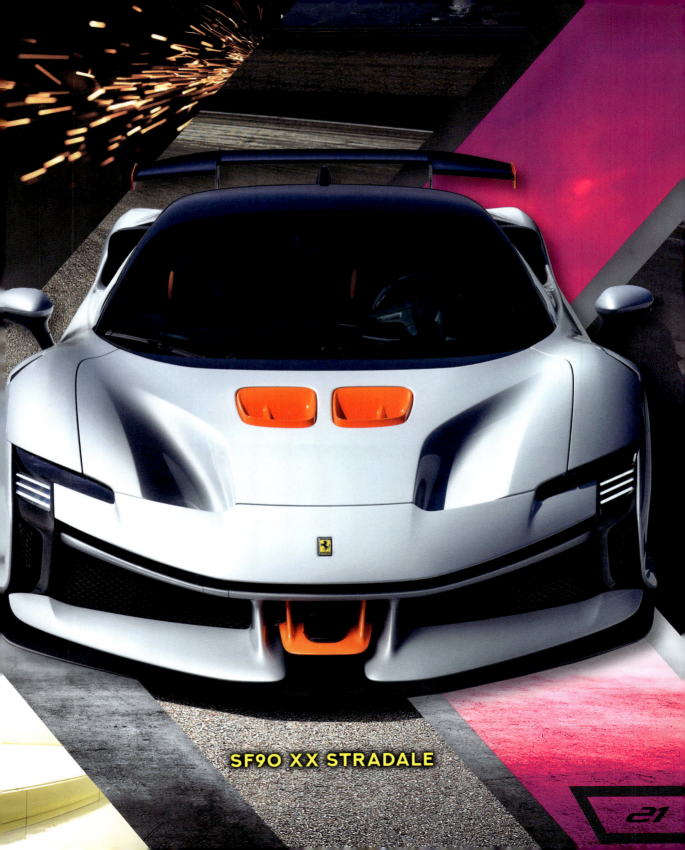

SF90 XX STRADALE

GLOSSARY

aerodynamic—able to move through air easily

air intakes—openings on a car that allow air to reach its engine

battery—a part that supplies electric energy to a car

convertible—a car with a folding or soft roof

electric motors—machines that give something the power to move by using electricity

Formula One—a type of car racing

head-up display—a display that shows images on a car's windshield so the driver can see them easily

horsepower—a measurement of the power of an engine or motor

hybrid—a car that uses both a gasoline engine and an electric motor for power

hypercar—an extreme, high-performing sports car that is expensive and made in a limited number

models—specific kinds of cars

spoiler—a part on the back of a car that helps the car grip the road

V8 engine—an engine with 8 cylinders arranged in the shape of a "V"

TO LEARN MORE

AT THE LIBRARY

Duling, Kaitlyn. *Ferrari 296 GTB*. Minneapolis, Minn.: Bellwether Media, 2024.

Emminizer, Theresa. *Ferraris*. Buffalo, N.Y.: Enslow Publishing, 2023.

Swanson, Jennifer. *How Do Hybrid Cars Work?* Mankato, Minn.: The Child's World, 2022.

ON THE WEB

FACTSURFER

Factsurfer.com gives you a safe, fun way to find more information.

1. Go to www.factsurfer.com.

2. Enter "Ferrari SF90 Stradale" into the search box and click 🔍.

3. Select your book cover to see a list of related content.

INDEX